LOVE

IS LIKE BREAD,

IT NEEDS TO BE

MADE FRESH

EVERYDAY!

Introduction

I assume you have purchased this book for the same reason I created it... I missed the taste and texture of traditional style bread; missed sandwiches, toast, the taste of sweet bread as a dessert.

Just because you are keto/ paleo/ gluten-free/ wheat-free, it doesn't mean you have to go without. Inside are twenty delicious gluten-free bread recipes that will have you forgetting about those high-carb refined grain breads in no time. They are all refined sugar-free, gluten-free and fit into a Paleo-style diet as well.

Most of the recipes are made from gluten-free flours such as almond flour and coconut. While these recipes contain healthier substitutions, they do not lack flavor!

There are a wide variety of breads to fill your bread cravings. You will find sweet loaf breads that serve as perfect dessert options or as a sweet treat for breakfast, sandwich breads so you can still enjoy your lunch time sandwich or morning toast, and dinner-style breads such as breadsticks.

There is also a fun section where you will find gluten-free bagels, pizza dough, tortillas and even gluten-free breadcrumbs. This book is for all the bread lovers out there who are looking for delicious ways to enjoy bread without indulging in gluten and excess sugar.

If you enjoyed this book, I'd appreciate it if you would leave a review. Simply visit http://geni.us/KetoBreadReview

EVERYTHING Bagels
GARLICKY
Pizza Dough

Making grain-free bread no longer has to be difficult, expensive or downright dry. I have created this recipe book full of 20 delicious grain-free breads in hopes of showing you that grain-free baking can be just as delicious as baking with wheat products.

I know how difficult grain-free baking can be. It's hard to know which flour to use, how much flour, and how much liquid and more times than not, the bread comes out dry and rock hard! Well, while creating these recipes I found the following tips to be very helpful on how to be a pro at grain-free baking. These baking tips have been around for a long time, but are not utilized that often. Many people have found shortcuts to make baking quicker and easier.

The thing is that in order to make a perfect grain-free bread, you need to take a little extra time to add the ingredients in the appropriate fashion to end up with an amazingly delicious bread. If you follow these steps you'll be wondering why you haven't been using them all along!

1. **Baking with coconut flour:** Coconut flour is great, but there's a trick to baking with this grain-free flour. In order to prevent your breads from coming out too dry, you will need to increase your eggs. Don't skimp on the eggs or you will be disappointed with the outcome. Most of the coconut flour recipes found in this book call for an average of 6 eggs. Just trust me in saying that all 6 are necessary for a moist and delicious grain-free bread!

   When purchasing coconut flour, you will also want to stay away from desiccated blends, as desiccated coconut flour still contains large amounts of coconut oil. In regular coconut flour, the flour contains much less oil which is ideal for baking the recipes in this book.

2. **Baking with almond flour:** If you are looking for a more traditionally tasting "grainy" bread, almond flour may be the best option for you. Almond flour also gives each recipe a delicious nutty flavor that pairs deliciously with flavors such as cinnamon, vanilla, and nutmeg. When cooking with almond flour, you don't need as many eggs as you would when cooking with coconut flour. Almond flour is not as absorbent as coconut flour, which is why you will not need as many eggs to make a moist bread. If you're looking for a heartier bread, I would recommend going with almond flour. Almond meal is a more coarsely ground flour which still contains the skin. Almond flour comes from blanched almonds (no skin) which results in a much finer flour.

3. **Always sift your coconut flour:** I cannot stress this enough! Not sifting your coconut flour will result in a grainy bread full of coconut flour clumps... yuck! To sift your coconut flour, simply use a mesh strainer, and add the coconut flour. Sift over a large container or bowl.

4. **Cream the sweetener and fat:** This is an old baking trick that many of us have forgotten to do! Instead of taking the shortcut, and pre-melting your coconut oil or butter, cream whatever fat you are using with the sweetener. By creaming your fat and sweetener, you will add air into the recipe which will result in a lighter end product. This is a necessity when using gluten-free baking flours.

5. **Use room temperature eggs:** Letting your eggs reach room temperature before baking allows the eggs to add a lighter texture to the final product.

6. **Add the eggs yolks to the creamed butter**: Instead of whisking the eggs separately, add the egg yolks into the already creamed fat and sweetener, and put the egg whites in a separate mixing bowl. You can also add the other ingredients after the egg yolks such as spices, gluten-free flour and baking powder, and blend.

7. **Whip the egg whites:** It's important to separate the egg yolks from the egg whites in order to create a lighter bread. You will want to whip the egg whites until stiff peaks form, preferably using a stand mixer. If you do not have a stand mixer, you can do so with a handheld mixer but this may take a little longer.

8. **Add the creamed fat mixture to the egg whites:** The last tip is to slowly fold the creamed fat mixture into the egg whites, and gently mix until combined. Do not over mix here, you want a fluffy consistency. Add to the prepped baking dish, and bake!

When you bake, and especially when you bake with grain-free flours, there is a method to how you should be mixing ingredients. If you mix them in this fashion, and you follow the flour and baking tips above, you will have a much better result, and a less grainy bread.

Baking Substitution Tips:

1. If a recipe calls for almond flour, but you wish to use coconut flour, you can easily make the swap. A good rule of thumb is to replace 1 cup of almond flour with ¼ cup of coconut flour. You will then need to adjust the liquid for the recipe which can be done by adding 1 egg for every ¼ cup of coconut flour in addition to the eggs the recipe originally called for.

2. If you want to add a nuttier flavor to a specific bread recipe, you can swap out the vanilla extract and use almond extract instead.

How This Book Works

This cookbook contains helpful baking tips so that you can make the most delicious gluten-free bread possible. There are also serving suggestions listed to give you an idea about what each of these breads pair well with. You will also notice that there is a difficulty level and cost scale listed on each recipe. Here is how to read both of these scales to determine the difficulty and price scale for each bread recipe.

Difficulty Level:

1. An easy-to-make bread that can be put together with just a handful of ingredients, and in a short amount of time.
2. These breads are a little more difficult and time consuming, but are still easy enough for even beginner bakers!
3. A more advanced bread for the adventurous baker! You will not see too many level 3 breads in this book, but there are a couple. These breads are great for when you have a little bit more time to spend in the kitchen, and when you want to make something out of the ordinary.

Cost:

$: A low budget everyday bread.

$$: A middle of the road, moderately-priced bread. The majority of the breads you will find in this book are considered a level $$ on the cost scale. These breads are not as cheap as level $, but they are still moderately priced and will not be as much as a level $$$.

$$$: A more expensive bread that is great for serving at a family gathering or party. These breads tend to contain pricey ingredients such as lots of nuts and seeds, but add a fabulous flavor to each recipe. You will not see too many level $$$ breads in this book, but there are a few that you can make to impress your guests with!

Let's Talk SWEETENERS

Before we get started, let's get down to business and talk sweeteners. When making grain-free, low-carb breads, you will notice that there are a couple of different natural sweetener options. These sweeteners take the place of sugar to add a hint of sweetness without excess carbs. In this book you will notice two different sweeteners being used, and I am going to briefly discuss the difference between the two.

1. **Erythritol:** Erythritol is great, because it can be used as a 1:1 substitution, meaning you can use the exact same amount of erythritol as you would sugar. Erythritol will provide you with just about the same amount of sweetness as regular sugar, which makes it the preferred natural sweetener among many low-carb bakers. This is a great natural sweetener to begin with if you are new to using them, as this sweetener seems to closely resemble sugar.

2. **Stevia:** Stevia is another natural sweetener found in the cookbook, and it is another great option for low-carb baking. Stevia extract is the extract of the stevia plant, which occurs naturally. This is a zero calorie sweetener, which makes it ideal for this type of baking. Stevia comes in both powder and liquid form. Liquid form is very easy to use, and you will only need to use a small amount since stevia is much sweetener than regular white sugar. There are also different liquid stevia flavors, which makes it an excellent choice to bring out different flavors in baking. In this book you will often see vanilla crème stevia extract being used. If you cannot find this particular stevia extract, you can use regular stevia and add a drop of additional pure vanilla extract.

BONUS KETO SWEET EATS SERIES

Thank you for downloading the book, I really appreciate it. I would like to return the favor. I am giving away the 'Keto Sweet Eats Series'. These are some of my favorite recipes including chocolate cake, ice cream, delightful fat bombs and more.

Simply visit the link below to get your free copy:

http://ketojane.com/sweets-b

BREAD & BUTTER

TRADITIONAL Sandwich Bread

DIFFICULTY LEVEL : 2  COST : $$ PREPARATION TIME : 15 MIN  COOKING TIME : 45 MIN  SERVES: 8

INGREDIENTS:

- ½ cup sifted coconut flour
- ¼ cup sifted gluten-free flour
- 6 room temperature eggs, separated
- ½ cup coconut oil
- 1 ½ teaspoons baking powder
- ¼ teaspoon salt
- 3 tablespoons water
- 1 tablespoon apple cider vinegar

NUTRITION FACTS (PER SERVING)
Total Carbs: 8g Fiber: 4g Protein: 6g Fat: 18g
Calories: 209 Net Carbs: 4g
% CALORIES FROM: Protein: 12% Fat: 80% Carbs: 8%

DIRECTIONS:

1. Preheat your oven to 350°F, grease an 8 ½ by 4 ½ loaf pan with oil, and place a piece of parchment paper on the bottom of the pan.
2. Start by creaming the coconut oil in a food processor. Add in the egg yolks one at a time, placing the egg whites into a separate mixing bowl. Pulse to combine the coconut oil and egg yolks.
3. Add in the sifted coconut and gluten-free flour, baking powder, apple cider vinegar, water and salt, and pulse one more time until combined.
4. In the mixing bowl beat the egg whites, with a handheld mixer until stiff peaks form.
5. Fold the coconut flour mixture into the egg whites, and mix just until combined.
6. Pour into the prepped loaf pan and bake for 40-45 minutes, covering with aluminum foil halfway through to prevent the top of the loaf from burning.
7. Allow the bread to cool in the pan for 15 minutes before slicing.
8. Cover and store in the fridge for 3–4 days

Serving suggestion: Use this bread as you would traditional sandwich bread. This bread is kid-approved and pairs great with peanut butter and jelly!

Baking tips: If you want to turn this into a cinnamon raisin bread, add 1 teaspoon of cinnamon and 2 tablespoons of raisins to the mix.

ALMOND Seed Bread

DIFFICULTY LEVEL : 3  COST : $$$  PREPARATION TIME : 2 HRS COOKING TIME : 50-75 MIN  SERVES: 8

INGREDIENTS:

- 1 cup hulled sunflower seeds
- 1 cup sliced almonds
- ½ cup chia seeds
- ½ cup psyllium husk (whole husk inc. seeds)
- 1 cup pumpkin seeds, divided into two ½ cup bowls
- 1 teaspoon salt
- ¼ cup coconut oil
- 1 ¼ cups water

NUTRITION FACTS (PER SERVING)

Total Carbs: 17g
Fiber: 12g
Protein: 14g
Fat: 35g
Calories: 406
Net Carbs: 3g

% CALORIES FROM:

Protein: 14%
Fat: 81%
Carbs: 5%

DIRECTIONS:

1. Start by toasting the ½ cup of pumpkin seeds, almonds, and sunflower seeds in a 325°F oven for 5 minutes.
2. While the seeds are toasting, combine the chia seeds, psyllium husk and salt in a large mixing bowl.
3. In a separate bowl, cream the coconut oil with a handheld mixer, and add it into the chia seeds mixture.
4. When the seeds are done toasting, turn off the oven, add the seeds into the mix, and stir. Add the water and continue to stir. If the bread seems dry, add 1 tablespoon of water at a time, you want the bread to stick together but without it being too watery.
5. Line a 9 by 5 loaf pan with coconut oil and parchment paper, and scoop the dough into the loaf pan. Top with additional pumpkin seeds and flatten. Cover the dough with a damp tea towel, and let it sit out for 2–3 hours before baking.
6. After 2–3 hours, preheat the oven to 375°F, and bake uncovered for 50 minutes to 1 hour and 15 minutes depending on your oven. Check the bread after 50 minutes. The bread will be done when it is golden brown.
7. Allow the bread to completely cool before removing it from the pan. This may take a couple of hours.
8. Slice and serve as you would traditional multigrain bread.

Serving suggestion: This bread pairs well with sliced avocado or sliced cheese.

Baking tips: You will know that the bread is cooked when it's golden brown. Be sure to check every 5 minutes when you reach that 50 minute mark to prevent overcooking the bread.

ALMOND Butter Bread

DIFFICULTY LEVEL : 2  COST : $$  PREPARATION TIME : 25 MIN COOKING TIME : 40 MIN  SERVES: 10

INGREDIENTS:

- 3 cups almond flour
- 3 room temperature eggs, separated
- 2 teaspoons quick rising yeast
- 1 teaspoon baking powder
- 1 teaspoon salt
- 2 teaspoons apple cider vinegar
- 2 tablespoons butter
- 2 tablespoons erythritol
- 1 cup plain full fat yogurt

NUTRITION FACTS (PER SERVING)
Total Carbs: 11g Fiber: 4g Protein: 10g Fat: 21g
Calories: 248 Net Carbs: 7g
% CALORIES FROM: Protein: 16% Fat: 74% Carbs: 11%

DIRECTIONS:

1. Preheat your oven to 350°F, grease a 10½ by 4 loaf pan with oil, and place a piece of parchment paper on the bottom of the pan.
2. Start by creaming the butter in a food processor. Add the egg yolks one at a time, placing the egg whites into a separate mixing bowl. Pulse to combine the butter and egg yolks.
3. Add the almond flour, plain yogurt, instant yeast, baking powder, apple cider vinegar, erythritol; and salt, and pulse one more time until combined.
4. Beat the egg whites, beat with a handheld mixer until stiff peaks form.
5. Fold the almond flour mixture into the egg whites, and mix just until combined. Let the dough sit in a loaf pan for 15 minutes to let it rise.
6. Bake for 40 minutes.
7. Allow the bread to cool in the pan for 15 minutes.
8. Turn the bread over onto a plate, and slice.
9. Store covered in the refrigerator to preserve freshness, and enjoy within a couple of days.

Serving suggestion: Use this bread as you would traditional sandwich bread, toasted with peanut butter or fresh butter.

Baking tips: If you want to make a seed bread, add pumpkin seeds into the mix before baking. You can also add crushed walnuts for a nuttier flavored bread. Add ground cinnamon, or nutmeg for a spiced bread flavor.

DINNER BREADS & ROLLS

DINNER Rolls

DIFFICULTY LEVEL : 1  COST : $$ PREPARATION TIME : 10 MIN  COOKING TIME : 20 MIN  SERVES: 10

INGREDIENTS:

- 6 eggs, separated
- ½ cup coconut flour
- ¼ cup psyllium husk (whole husk inc. seeds)
- 1 tablespoon garlic powder
- ½ teaspoon salt
- 1 teaspoon apple cider vinegar
- 6 tablespoons butter
- 1 ½ teaspoons baking powder

NUTRITION FACTS (PER SERVING)
Total Carbs: 6g Fiber: 3g Protein: 4g Fat: 10g
Calories: 130 Net Carbs: 3g

% CALORIES FROM: Protein: 14% Fat: 76% Carbs: 10%

DIRECTIONS:

1. Preheat your oven to 350°F, and line a baking sheet with parchment paper.
2. Start by creaming the butter and adding in 1 egg yolk at a time, placing the egg whites into a separate bowl.
3. Add the remaining ingredients into the butter and egg mixture, and mix until combined. Set aside.
4. Whip the egg whites with a stand mixer or a handheld mixer until stiff peaks form. Fold the butter mix into the egg whites. Mix until just combined.
5. Form into 10 rolls, and bake for 20 minutes.
6. Enjoy while warm!

Serving suggestion: Serve with a salad, or as an appetizer with marinara sauce or olive oil.

Baking tips: Add seasoning of choice if desired. Oregano, red pepper flakes, or onion powder are great options for this recipe.

CORNBREAD Muffins

DIFFICULTY LEVEL : 1  **COST : $$** **PREPARATION TIME : 10 MIN**  **COOKING TIME : 20 MIN**  **SERVES: 6**

INGREDIENTS:

- ¾ cup almond flour
- ¼ cup gluten-free cornmeal
- 1 teaspoon baking powder
- ½ teaspoon salt
- 2 eggs
- 4 tablespoons butter
- ¼ cup full fat unsweetened yogurt

NUTRITION FACTS (PER SERVING)
Total Carbs: 8g Fiber: 2g Protein: 6g Fat: 17g
Calories: 194 Net Carbs: 6g

% CALORIES FROM: Protein: 12% Fat: 76% Carbs: 12%

DIRECTIONS:

1. Preheat your oven to 350°F, and grease a muffin tin with coconut oil.
2. Start by creaming the butter and adding in 1 egg yolk at a time, placing the egg whites into a separate bowl.
3. Add the remaining ingredients into the butter and egg mixture, and mix until combined. Set aside.
4. Whip the egg whites with a stand mixer or a handheld mixer until stiff peaks form. Fold the butter mix into the egg whites. Mix until just combined.
5. Pour the batter into the muffin tins, and bake for 20 minutes or until the tops of the muffins are golden brown.
6. Enjoy while warm!

Serving suggestion: Serve with a slab of butter as an appetizer or serve alongside a main meal.

Baking tips: Omit the cornmeal and add in ¼ more cup of almond flour, if desired.

CHEESY BREADSTICKS

DIFFICULTY LEVEL : 1 **COST : $$** **PREPARATION TIME : 10 MIN**  **COOKING TIME : 20 MIN**  **SERVES: 13 (1 BREADSTICK EACH)**

INGREDIENTS:

- 2 cups of shredded mozzarella cheese
- 2 Tbsp. coconut flour
- 2 eggs
- 1 pinch of salt

Toppings:

- ½ cup of shredded parmesan cheese
- 1 Tbsp. Italian seasoning
- ½ tsp. garlic powder

NUTRITION FACTS (PER SERVING)
Total Carbs: 2g Fiber: 1g Protein: 4g Fat: 3g
Calories: 47 Net Carbs: 1g

% CALORIES FROM: Protein: 34% Fat: 57% Carbs: 9%

DIRECTIONS:

1. Start by preheating the oven to 350 degrees F and lining a baking sheet with parchment paper.
2. Next, add the mozzarella cheese, coconut flour, eggs, and salt to a food processor and process until smooth.
3. Scoop the mixture onto the lined baking sheet and flatten to about 1-inch thick forming a square.
4. Bake for 15 minutes.
5. Remove from the oven and sprinkle with the parmesan cheese, Italian seasoning, and garlic, powder.
6. Bake for an additional 5 minutes or until the parmesan cheese is melted.
7. Remove from the oven and allow the breadsticks to cool for 10-15 minutes before slicing.

Cooking/Serving Suggestions: Use a pizza cutter to slice into breadsticks. Store covered in the fridge for a couple of days and reheat in the oven for 10-minutes before serving.

LOAF BREADS

Spiced Zucchini Bread

Sweet Potato Bread

Cinnamon Swirl Bread

Almond Pumpkin Seed Bread

Blueberry Loaf

Decadent Chocolate Loaf Bread

Lemon Bread

SPICED Zucchini Bread

DIFFICULTY LEVEL : 2  COST : $$ PREPARATION TIME : 15 MIN  COOKING TIME : 40 MIN  SERVES: 6

INGREDIENTS:

- ⅔ cup coconut flour
- 2 tablespoons gluten-free flour
- 3 eggs, separated
- ¼ cup melted butter
- ⅔ cup shredded zucchini
- ⅔ cup coconut milk
- 1 teaspoon allspice
- 1 teaspoon cinnamon
- ¼ teaspoon salt
- ½ teaspoon pure vanilla extract
- 1 teaspoon baking powder
- ¼ cup erythritol

DIRECTIONS:

1. Preheat your oven to 400°F, grease a loaf pan with oil, and place a piece of parchment paper on the bottom of the pan.
2. Whisk the coconut flour with the spices and baking powder. In a separate bowl, beat the eggs with the butter until pale. Pour in the coconut cream and whisk to combine. Add the wet ingredients to the dry mixture and stir with a wooden spoon until no lumps remain.
3. Squeeze any excess moisture out of the shredded zucchini and add it to the batter. Mix just until combined. Pour into the baking pan.
4. Bake for 40 minutes or until a toothpick inserted into the center of the bread comes out clean.

NUTRITION FACTS (PER SERVING)
Total Carbs: 13g Fiber: 7g Protein: 6g Fat: 17g
Calories: 228 Net Carbs: 5g

% CALORIES FROM: Protein: 12% Fat: 78% Carbs: 10%

Sweet Potato Bread

DIFFICULTY LEVEL : 2  COST : $$  PREPARATION TIME : 15 MIN  COOKING TIME : 20 MIN  SERVES: 6

INGREDIENTS:

- ¼ cup coconut flour
- 3 eggs, separated
- 2 tablespoons softened butter
- 2 tablespoons coconut milk (canned)
- ¼ teaspoon salt
- ½ teaspoon pure vanilla extract
- ¼ teaspoon baking powder
- ½ cup pureed sweet potato (fresh or store bought)
- ¼ cup walnuts
- 1 teaspoon vanilla crème stevia extract

NUTRITION FACTS (PER SERVING)
Total Carbs: 7g Fiber: 3g Protein: 5g Fat: 11g
Calories: 143 Net Carbs: 4g

% CALORIES FROM: Protein: 15% Fat: 73% Carbs: 12%

DIRECTIONS:

1. Preheat your oven to 400°F, grease a loaf pan with oil, and place a piece of parchment paper on the bottom of the pan.
2. Cream the butter and stevia together. Add the egg yolks and mix, placing the whites in a separate bowl. Add the remaining ingredients minus the walnuts, and mix again. Gently fold in the walnuts last.
3. Whisk the egg whites with a handheld or stand mixer until stiff peaks form, and fold the butter mixture into the eggs. Mix just until combined. Pour into the baking pan.
4. Bake for 20 minutes or until a toothpick inserted into the center of the bread comes out clean.

CINNAMON Swirl Bread

DIFFICULTY LEVEL : 2 COST : $$ PREPARATION TIME : 15 MIN COOKING TIME : 40 MIN SERVES: 8

INGREDIENTS:

- ½ cup of coconut flour
- 6 eggs
- ½ cup butter
- ½ cup erythritol
- 1 tablespoon erythritol (for cinnamon swirl)
- ½ teaspoon pure vanilla extract
- 1 teaspoon baking powder
- 1 teaspoon cinnamon

Cinnamon Swirl:

- 1 tablespoon erythritol mixed with 1 tablespoon cinnamon

NUTRITION FACTS (PER SERVING)
Total Carbs: 19g Fiber: 3g Protein: 5g Fat: 16g
Calories: 183 Net Carbs: 16g

% CALORIES FROM: Protein: 9% Fat: 63% Carbs: 28%

DIRECTIONS:

1. Preheat your oven to 350°F, and grease a loaf pan with coconut oil. You will also want to line the loaf pan with parchment paper, as this bread tends to stick.
2. Start making the cinnamon swirl by mixing the 1 tablespoon of erythritol plus the 1 teaspoon of cinnamon together in a bowl, and set aside.
3. Cream the butter and ½ cup of erythritol together. Add the egg yolks and mix, placing the whites in a separate bowl. Add the remaining ingredients and mix again.
4. In a separate bowl, whisk the egg whites with a handheld or stand mixer until stiff peaks form. Fold the butter mixture into the whisked egg whites. Mix just until combined.
5. Pour half of the batter into the loaf pan, and top with half of the cinnamon swirl mixture. Top this half with the remaining bread batter, and smooth the batter out evenly.
6. Add the remaining cinnamon swirl mixture on top of the loaf and swirl.
7. Bake for 40 minutes, or until the bread is set.
8. Allow to cool in the pan before slicing.

ALMOND Pumpkin Seed Bread

DIFFICULTY LEVEL : 2  COST : $$  PREPARATION TIME : 15 MIN COOKING TIME : 35-40 MIN  SERVES: 8

INGREDIENTS:

- 6 eggs, beaten
- ½ cup melted coconut oil
- 1 teaspoon vanilla extract
- ¼ cup erythritol
- ½ cup coconut flour, sifted
- ½ teaspoon salt
- ½ teaspoon baking powder
- 1 tablespoon pumpkin pie spice
- 1 teaspoon cinnamon
- ½ cup slivered almonds
- ½ cup pumpkin seeds, divided into two ¼ cup bowls

NUTRITION FACTS (PER SERVING)
Total Carbs: 13g Fiber: 4g Protein: 9g Fat: 25g
Calories: 282 Net Carbs: 9g

% CALORIES FROM: Protein: 12% Fat: 76% Carbs: 12%

DIRECTIONS:

1. Preheat your oven to 350°F, and grease a loaf pan with coconut oil. For best results, line the loaf pan with parchment paper to prevent the bread from sticking.
2. Cream the coconut oil and erythritol together. Add the egg yolks and mix, placing the egg whites in a separate bowl. Add the remaining ingredients, minus the pumpkin seeds, the slivered almonds, and the egg whites, and mix again. Gently fold in the slivered almonds and half of the pumpkin seeds last.
3. Whisk the egg whites with a handheld or stand mixer until stiff peaks form, and fold the flour mixture into the eggs. Mix just until combined. Pour into the baking pan.
4. Bake for 35–40 minutes, or until the middle of the loaf is set and a toothpick inserted into the center of the bread comes out clean.
5. Once the bread is finished baking, add the remaining ¼ cup pumpkin seeds to the outside of the bread by gently pressing the pumpkin seeds into the bread as best as you can. It's okay if many of them fall off, this is just to add some additional crunch to the bread.
6. Allow the bread to cool for 15 minutes before serving.

Serving suggestion: I recommend serving this bread warm. To serve leftover bread, simply microwave or re-heat it in the oven and serve with a slab of butter.

Baking tips: If you want to bring out the pumpkin and cinnamon flavors, add in a pinch of nutmeg. Also, stevia can be used in place of erythritol, but you will only need about 1 teaspoon of liquid stevia, as stevia is much sweeter.

BLUEBERRY Loaf

DIFFICULTY LEVEL : 2 $COST : $$  PREPARATION TIME : 15 MIN  COOKING TIME : 35-40 MIN  SERVES: 8

INGREDIENTS:

- ½ cup coconut flour
- 6 eggs
- ½ cup butter
- 8 teaspoons erythritol
- ½ teaspoon salt
- ½ teaspoon pure vanilla extract
- 1 teaspoon baking powder
- ½ cup fresh blueberries (not frozen)

NUTRITION FACTS (PER SERVING)
Total Carbs: 9g Fiber: 3g Protein: 5g Fat: 4g
Calories: 81 Net Carbs: 6g

% CALORIES FROM: Protein: 25% Fat: 45% Carbs: 30%

DIRECTIONS:

1. Preheat your oven to 350°F, and grease a loaf pan with coconut oil or butter. You will also want to line the loaf pan with parchment paper so you can easily remove the loaf from the pan after cooking.
2. Cream the butter and erythritol together. Add the egg yolks and mix, placing the egg whites in a separate bowl. Add the remaining ingredients, minus the blueberries and mix again. Gently fold in the blueberries last.
3. Whisk the egg whites with a handheld or stand mixer until stiff peaks form, and fold the flour mixture into the eggs. Mix just until combined. Pour into the baking pan.
4. Bake for 35–40 minutes, or until a toothpick inserted in the center comes out clean.
5. Allow the bread to cool for 15 minutes before serving.

Serving suggestion: This bread works as an excellent on-the-go breakfast, or even as an after dinner treat. I recommend serving this with a cup of coffee or herbal tea. To turn this into a dessert, try topping the bread with a dollop of unsweetened whipped cream. Please note that any addition to the bread is not reflected in the nutritional information.

Baking tips: If you want a more "grainy" and nutty flavored bread, you can sub out the coconut flour for almond flour. Increase to 1 ¼ cups almond flour instead of ½ cup coconut flour, and 2 eggs instead of 6. Stevia can be used in place of erythritol, but you will only need about 1 teaspoon of liquid stevia as stevia is much sweeter.

DECADENT Chocolate Loaf Bread

DIFFICULTY LEVEL : 2 $ COST : $$  PREPARATION TIME : 20 MIN  COOKING TIME : 40 MIN  SERVES: 12

INGREDIENTS:

- ½ cup of coconut flour
- 6 eggs
- 1 cup mashed avocado
- ½ cup butter, melted
- ½ cup erythritol
- ¼ cup raw unsweetened cocoa powder
- ½ teaspoon pure vanilla extract
- 1 teaspoon baking powder
- Coconut oil for greasing

NUTRITION FACTS (PER SERVING)
Total Carbs: 13g Fiber: 2g Protein: 4g Fat: 13g
Calories: 132 Net Carbs: 11g
% CALORIES FROM: Protein: 9% Fat: 66% Carbs: 25%

DIRECTIONS:

1. Preheat your oven to 350°F, and grease a loaf pan with coconut oil. You will also want to line the loaf pan with parchment paper, as this bread tends to stick.
2. Cream the butter and 1/2 cup of erythritol together. Add the egg yolks and mix, placing the whites in a separate bowl. Add the remaining ingredients and mix again.
3. In a separate bowl, whisk the egg whites with a handheld or stand mixer until stiff peaks form. Fold the butter mixture into the whisked egg whites. Mix just until combined.
4. Bake for 40 minutes, or until the bread is set. Allow to cool in the pan before slicing.

Serving suggestion: To turn this into more of a dessert-style bread, top the loaf with additional dark chocolate chips and a dollop of unsweetened whipped cream. Please note that this is not reflected in the nutritional information. Store the bread in the refrigerator to keep it fresh, and re-heat as desired.

LEMON Bread

DIFFICULTY LEVEL : 2 **COST : $$** **PREPARATION TIME : 15 MIN** **COOKING TIME : 35-40 MIN** **SERVES: 6**

INGREDIENTS:

- ½ cup coconut flour (sifted)
- ¼ cup butter
- 6 eggs, separated
- Juice from 2 lemons
- ¾ cup full fat coconut milk
- ¼ cup erythritol
- ½ teaspoon pure vanilla extract
- 1 teaspoon baking powder
- ½ teaspoon salt

NUTRITION FACTS (PER SERVING)
Total Carbs: 17g Fiber: 4g Protein: 8g Fat: 20g
Calories: 244 Net Carbs: 13g

% CALORIES FROM: Protein: 12% Fat: 68% Carbs: 20%

DIRECTIONS:

1. Preheat your oven to 350°F, grease a loaf pan with oil, and place a piece of parchment paper on the bottom of the pan.
2. Cream the butter and erythritol together. Add the egg yolks and mix, placing the egg whites in a separate bowl. Add the remaining ingredients, and mix again.
3. Whisk the egg whites with a handheld or stand mixer until stiff peaks form, and fold the butter mixture into the eggs. Mix just until combined. Pour into the baking pan.
4. Bake for 35–40 minutes or until a toothpick inserted into the center of the bread comes out clean.
5. Allow the loaf to cool before slicing.

Serving suggestion: Serve as a yummy breakfast bread with a cup of coffee or tea.

Baking tips: Check the bread at the 35 minute mark. You want to be sure that the top of the bread does not burn, so remove from the oven when golden brown.

REWORKED CLASSICS

Everything Bagels

Microwave Cinnamon English Muffins

Cloud Bread

Garlicky Pizza Dough

No Flour Tortillas

Pumpkin Bread Muffins

Italian-Style Breadcrumbs

Rustic Boule

Jalapeño Cornbread

EVERYTHING Bagels

DIFFICULTY LEVEL : 2  COST : $$ PREPARATION TIME : 25 MIN  COOKING TIME : 15-20 MIN  SERVES: 6

INGREDIENTS:

- 2 cups almond flour
- 1 cup gluten-free flour
- 1 egg
- ¼ cup sifted coconut flour
- 2 teaspoons instant rise yeast
- 2 tablespoons olive oil
- 6 tablespoons hot water
- 4 cups cold water
- 1 teaspoon baking soda
- 1 teaspoon melted butter
- 2 tablespoons poppy seeds
- 1 tablespoon granulated onion
- 1 tablespoon granulated garlic
- Pinch of sea salt

NUTRITION FACTS (PER SERVING)
Total Carbs: 19g Fiber: 3g Protein: 5g Fat: 16g
Calories: 183 Net Carbs: 16g

% CALORIES FROM: Protein: 9% Fat: 63% Carbs: 28%

DIRECTIONS:

1. In a large mixing bowl, whisk together the 6 tablespoons of hot water, the olive oil; and the yeast.
2. Whisk the egg in a large separate mixing bowl, then add the almond flour, gluten-free flour, garlic and onion. Mix well and then add the water, oil and yeast mixture, and combine to form a dough. Form into 6 balls, and shape into bagels.
3. Add the 4 cups of cold water, salt and baking soda to a large pot and bring to a boil. Preheat your oven to 350°F, and line a baking sheet with parchment paper.
4. Once the water is boiling, add one bagel at a time. Boil each one for about 1 minute and then transfer it to the baking sheet. Brush with the melted butter, sprinkle with the poppy seeds, and bake for about 15 minutes or until crispy.

Serving suggestion: Serve with cream cheese or butter as you would a traditional bagel.

Baking tips: You can make the bagels in any flavor you desire. Delicious options include cinnamon or sesame bagels.

MICROWAVE Cinnamon English Muffins

DIFFICULTY LEVEL : 1  COST : $ PREPARATION TIME : 10 MIN  COOKING TIME : 3-5 MIN  SERVES: 2

INGREDIENTS:

- 2 tablespoons coconut flour, sifted
- 2 tablespoons unsweetened soy milk
- 2 eggs
- 1 tablespoon butter
- 1 tablespoon coconut oil
- ½ teaspoon baking powder
- ¼ teaspoon apple cider vinegar
- 1 teaspoon ground cinnamon
- 1 pinch of sea salt

NUTRITION FACTS (PER SERVING)
Total Carbs: 6g Fiber: 3g Protein: 7g Fat: 18g
Calories: 214 Net Carbs: 3g
% CALORIES FROM: Protein: 14% Fat: 80% Carbs: 6%

DIRECTIONS:

1. Start by melting the butter together with the coconut oil and soy milk in a microwave-safe dish, and whisk.
2. In a separate bowl, whisk together the flour, baking powder, apple cider vinegar, cinnamon, and salt. Add the egg yolks and whip. Pour into the melted butter mixture and mix.
3. In a separate bowl, whip the egg whites with a handheld mixer until stiff peaks form, and gently fold into the flour mixture.
4. Pour batter into 2 greased ramekin dishes, filling them halfway, and microwave for about 1 minute or until the center of the English muffin is set.
5. Cool for a couple of minutes, and then remove from the dish and slice.
6. Toast if desired, and serve with butter or ghee (optional).

Serving suggestion: Make an egg sandwich using these delicious homemade and grain-free English muffins.

Baking tips: You will know the English muffins are cooked when the center has set. If it's not done within the 1 minute cooking time, cook for an additional 20 seconds until done.

CLOUD Bread

DIFFICULTY LEVEL : 1 | COST : $ |  PREPARATION TIME : 15 MIN |  COOKING TIME : 30 MIN |  SERVES: 10

INGREDIENTS:

- 3 eggs, separated
- 3 tablespoons butter
- ¼ teaspoon apple cider vinegar
- 1 drop stevia extract
- ½ teaspoon baking powder
- 1 pinch of salt

DIRECTIONS:

1. Preheat your oven to 300°F, and line a baking sheet with parchment paper.
2. Place the egg yolks in one bowl, and the egg whites in another. In the bowl with the yolks, whisk the eggs and add the remaining ingredients.
3. Whip the egg whites with a stand or handheld mixer until stiff peaks form. Fold the egg yolk mixture into the egg whites, and very gently combine.
4. Form into 10 rounds, and place on the baking sheet.
5. Bake for about 30 minutes or until golden brown.
6. Enjoy warm, and store the leftovers covered in the refrigerator.

Serving suggestion: Serve alongside a salad or with a bowl of soup.

Baking tips: You will want to be very careful not to overmix the egg yolk mixture into the egg whites as doing so will lead to a less fluffy bread.

GARLICKY Pizza Dough

DIFFICULTY LEVEL : 1 $COST : $  PREPARATION TIME : 10 MIN  COOKING TIME : 20 MIN  SERVES: 4

INGREDIENTS:

- 1 cup almond flour
- ½ cup gluten-free flour
- 3 garlic cloves
- 2 eggs
- 2 tablespoons olive oil
- 1 teaspoon baking powder
- 1 pinch of salt

DIRECTIONS:

1. Preheat your oven to 400°F, and line a baking sheet with parchment paper.
2. Add all of the ingredients together in a high speed blender, and blend until smooth.
3. Place the dough onto the parchment-lined baking sheet, and roll into a long rectangular shape, or shape into a traditional circular pizza.
4. Bake for 10 minutes, or until lightly browned. Then, sprinkle with your topping of choice, and bake for 10 more minutes.

Serving suggestions: Add your favorite pizza toppings such as cheese, green peppers, onion, and sausage.

Baking tips: If the dough seems too dry, add 1 more tablespoon of olive oil to thin. This dough makes more of a savory-flavored pizza than a traditional pizza, so feel free to add all sorts of fancy toppings such as mushrooms or a sharp tasting cheese, such as feta cheese, or even some fresh herbs.

NO FLOUR Tortillas

DIFFICULTY LEVEL : 2  **COST : $** **PREPARATION TIME : 5 MIN**  **COOKING TIME : APPROXIMATELY 10-15 MIN**
SERVES: 12 (1 TORTILLA PER SERVING)

INGREDIENTS:

- ½ cup softened cream cheese
- 6 eggs
- ½ cup whole milk
- 1 tsp. garlic powder
- Pinch of salt
- Coconut oil for cooking (not reflected in nutritional information)

NUTRITION FACTS (PER SERVING)
Total Carbs: 1g Fiber: 0g Protein: 4g Fat: 6g
Calories: 72 Net Carbs: 1g
% CALORIES FROM: Protein: 22% Fat: 73% Carbs: 5%

DIRECTIONS:

1. Start by preheating a small omelet sized skillet over medium heat with coconut oil.
2. Add all the ingredients to a food processor and process until smooth.
3. Pour just enough batter to cover the bottom of the skillet and cook for 45-1 minute on each side.
4. Repeat this process until all of the tortillas are cooked using additional coconut oil each time to prevent sticking.

Cooking Suggestions: These cook fast so flip each tortilla quickly once the center starts to set. Serve as you would a traditional tortilla.

PUMPKIN Bread Muffins

DIFFICULTY LEVEL : 2  COST : $$  PREPARATION TIME : 18 MIN COOKING TIME : 18 MIN  SERVES: 8

INGREDIENTS:

- ½ cup coconut flour, sifted
- ½ cup canned pumpkin puree
- 3 tablespoons butter OR coconut oil (butter reflected in nutritional information)
- 6 eggs, separated
- 1 teaspoon pumpkin pie spice
- 1 teaspoon pure vanilla extract
- ¼ cup erythritol
- 1 teaspoon baking powder
- ½ teaspoon salt
- ¼ cup walnuts, chopped

NUTRITION FACTS (PER SERVING)

Total Carbs: 12g
Fiber: 3g
Protein: 6g
Fat: 11g
Calories: 148
Net Carbs: 9g

% CALORIES FROM:

Protein: 15%
Fat: 62%
Carbs: 23%

DIRECTIONS:

1. Preheat your oven to 350°F, and grease a muffin tin with coconut oil.
2. Cream the butter and erythritol together. Add the egg yolks and mix, placing the whites in a separate bowl. Add the remaining ingredients and mix again.
3. Whisk the egg whites with a handheld or stand mixer until stiff peaks form, and fold the pumpkin mixture into the eggs. Mix just until combined. Pour into the muffin tins.
4. Bake for 18–20 minutes or until a toothpick inserted into the center of the muffins comes out clean.

Serving suggestion: Serve with a slab of butter and a hot cup of coffee for the perfect fall breakfast.

Baking tips: For a nuttier flavor, replace the coconut flour with 1 ¼ cups of almond flour, and reduce the eggs to 3.

ITALIAN-STYLE Breadcrumbs

DIFFICULTY LEVEL : 2  COST : $$  PREPARATION TIME : 18 MIN COOKING TIME : 18 MIN  SERVES: 8

INGREDIENTS:

- 1 cup almond meal
- 2 tablespoons dried parmesan cheese
- 1 teaspoon garlic powder
- ½ teaspoon onion powder
- ½ teaspoon dried oregano
- ½ teaspoon dried rosemary
- ¼ teaspoon black pepper
- ½ teaspoon salt

NUTRITION FACTS (PER SERVING)
Total Carbs: 3g Fiber: 1g Protein: 3g Fat: 6g
Calories: 70 Net Carbs: 2g
% CALORIES FROM: Protein: 16% Fat: 73% Carbs:11%

DIRECTIONS:

1. Add all of the ingredients to a large mixing bowl, and stir to combine.
2. Store in an airtight container in the refrigerator.

Serving suggestion: Use as you would traditional breadcrumbs. Use to bread chicken or even vegetables for a delicious breaded zucchini. Toss on salads for a nutty Italian flavor, or use on top of casseroles.

Baking tips: Use these breadcrumbs as you would bake with traditional breadcrumbs. To bread chicken, dip the chicken in a bowl of whisked eggs, and then in the homemade breadcrumbs for a healthy, gluten-free alternative to standard store - bought breadcrumbs.

Rustic Boule

DIFFICULTY LEVEL : 1 **COST : $** **PREPARATION TIME : 20 MIN + 1 HOUR PROVING TIME**

COOKING TIME : 35-40 MIN **SERVES: 12**

INGREDIENTS:

- 1 ½ cup coconut milk 375ml (~55g)
- ½ teaspoon powdered stevia
- 2 teaspoon dry yeast
- 2 eggs, room temperature
- 1 teaspoon apple cider vinegar
- 1 cup almond flour, sifted 110g
- 2 cups gluten-free all-purpose flour, sifted
- ½ teaspoon salt
- 3 tablespoon olive oil.

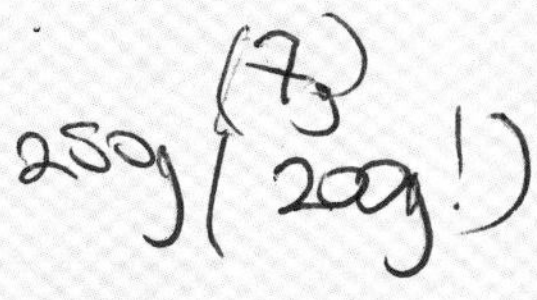

NUTRITION FACTS (PER SERVING)
Total Carbs: 10g Fiber: 3g Protein: 1g Fat: 13g
Calories: 161 Net Carbs: 7g
% CALORIES FROM: Protein: 3% Fat: 79% Carbs:19%

DIRECTIONS:

1. Preheat your oven to 400°F, and line a baking sheet with parchment paper.
2. Warm the coconut milk over a low heat, then add the stevia and yeast, and whisk to combine.
3. In a separate bowl, whisk the room temperature eggs with apple cider vinegar. Pour in the warm milk and whisk again to combine.
4. Mix both the almond and gluten-free flours with the salt. Add the wet ingredients, including 2 ½ tablespoons of the olive oil, and mix well. Knead the dough until it comes together. It should be a little sticky, but feel free to add more gluten-free flour if it's too sticky.
5. Shape the dough into a ball on the parchment-lined baking sheet. Brush with the rest of the olive oil and cover with plastic wrap. Let it prove in a warm place for an hour.
6. Remove the plastic wrap, dust with a small handful of gluten-free flour and bake for 35-40 minutes.

JALAPEÑO Cornbread

DIFFICULTY LEVEL : 1  COST : $ PREPARATION TIME : 10 MIN  COOKING TIME : 30 MIN  SERVES: 6

INGREDIENTS:

- 1 cup gluten-free all-purpose flour
- 1 cup gluten-free cornmeal
- 1 ½ teaspoon baking powder
- 1 teaspoon baking soda
- 1 teaspoon salt
- 1 cup buttermilk
- 2 eggs
- 2 tablespoon olive oil
- ¼ teaspoon stevia extract
- 1 jalapeno pepper, finely chopped

NUTRITION FACTS (PER SERVING)
Total Carbs: 7g Fiber: 1g Protein: 1g Fat: 4g
Calories:74 Net Carbs: 6g
% CALORIES FROM: Protein: 6% Fat: 56% Carbs:38%

DIRECTIONS:

1. Grease a cast iron skillet and preheat your oven to 350°F.
2. Setting the chopped jalapeño aside, whisk the rest of the wet and dry ingredients in separate mixing bowls, then combine and stir until smooth. Add the chopped jalapeño and stir well to mix it evenly through the bread.
3. Pour the mixture into the greased cast iron skillet and bake in the oven for 30-35 minutes.
4. Let the bread cool before slicing and serving.

Serving suggestion: Top with freshly sliced jalapeños for an extra kick.

...UK-US CONVERSION Chart...

Spoon, Cups & Liquid

Spoon, Cups & Liquid	ml
¼ tsp	1.25 ml
½ tsp	2.5 ml
1 tsp	5 ml
1 tbsp	15 ml
¼ cup	60 ml
⅓ cup	80 ml
½ cup	125 ml
1 cup	250 ml

Temperature

Gas Mark	°C	°F
1	140 °C	275 °F
2	150 °C	300 °F
3	170 °C	325 °F
4	180 °C	350 °F
5	190 °C	375 °F
6	200 °C	400°F
7	220 °C	425 °F
8	230 °C	450 °F
9	240 °C	475 °F

American Cups to Grams

Ingredients	Grams	Ingredients	Grams
1 cup butter	225g	1 cup raising/sutanas	200g
1 stick butter	113g	1 cup currants	150g
1 cup flour	125g	1 cup ground almonds	110g
1 cup white sugar	225g	1 cup syrup	350g
1 cup brown sugar	200g	1 cup rice (uncooked)	200g
1 cup icing sugar	125g		

YOU MAY ALSO LIKE...

To view all the other delicious books by the author, visit the link below.

http://ketojane.com/books

For permissions contact:

elizabeth@elizjanehealthy.com or visit http://ketojane.com/

Printed in Great Britain
by Amazon